ODE TO JOY

Also by John R. McDonough

Books of Poetry

Casting About: 100 Lyric Poems from the Heart

The Open Door

Winter Sun

beatitude: New and Selected Poems

Then

Thence

Memoirs and Books of Prose

The Good Doctor: A Memoir

Angels and Other Stories

Daddy, Tell us a Story: A Memoir

Through a Porthole: WWII in the Pacific

ODE TO JOY

*For
Joe Galagan
many Thanks !!*

JOHN R. MCDONOUGH

John R. McDonough

ISBN: 9798305570366
Library of Congress Control Number: 2025930616

Printed in the United States of America

DEDICATION

To those who long for:
Love, joy, peace, patience, kindness, goodness, faith,
modesty, and continence

And wish to avoid:
Immorality, uncleanness, licentiousness, idolatry,
witchcrafts, enmities, contentions, jealousies, anger,
quarrels, factions, orgies, envies, murders,
drunkenness, carousing, and suchlike.
(Galatians 5: 18-24)

Then:
Ask and it shall be given you; seek and you shall find;
Knock, and it shall be opened to you.
For everyone who asks, receives; and he who seeks, finds;
and to him who knocks, it shall be opened.
(Matthew: 8: 7-9)

TABLE OF CONTENTS

FOREWORD

John McDonough has returned in one of his most ambitious projects to date - a celebration of Christianity in verse. And a celebration it is, with its watchword "joy."

He has adopted as his theme and model, Friedrich Schiller's "Ode to Joy." McDonough's poem, too, is an ode, a celebration, from the Immaculate Conception through the founding of the Church, with special attention to the legacy of Christianity's spiritual gifts.

McDonough promises to present this ode "from the perspective of a physician and father of seven children." And he delivers.

Some of the verses closely follow the text of well-known biblical events. But some are, as John promises, quite medical in their focus. He draws attention to Mary's "bulge," since only someone who is not a doctor would find a way to ignore such a thing. And he includes an entire verse entitled "Afterbirth." Then, even though Jesus's presentation at the temple after eight days is universally understood to include his circumcision, here too McDonough makes the assumption overt, and even gives us a glimpse of Jesus under the knife.

And then there is the emphasis on the family. The Bible largely glosses over Jesus's childhood, with the exception of his presentation at the temple and his later wandering off on his own to teach at the temple. But McDonough devotes a canto to speculation (and is clear that it is merely speculation) as to what may have happened during that time with regard to his education, his upbringing, even his childhood friends, bringing us some of the "dirt and grime" of living in the world.

There are also the more familiar aspects of Jesus's public ministry. His teachings. The miracles. But Mc-Donough manages to find a lens through which to shine new light onto these. Consider the Transfiguration. Instead of merely focusing on the blinding vision of Jesus with the prophets, McDonough also uses it as an opportunity for a meditation on time and aging:

> Oh to turn the clock back on then
> Add some years be young again
> Yet we know that we cannot but
> Capture time with ink and pen

The poem gives ample attention to recounting the Passion and Resurrection, but for McDonough, and for us, this is hardly the end. In fact, it might be said that all the previous cantos and the verses within them are only there to make the final several cantos possible. And it is in enumeration of the blessings that all of this has left us - the gifts of the Holy Spirit, the fruits of the Holy Spirit, the sacraments, the great figures of the early church, the cardinal virtues - that McDonough's ode lavishes its praise. And even all this, he reminds us, is preparation for the life to come.

One of the difficulties in writing a narrative poem is to keep the story moving along, while remaining confined by the poem's structure. It has to fit the structure (rhyme, meter, number of stanzas). McDonough achieves this by treating each event as a verse. McDonough largely achieves this by relying on the biblical account, but occasionally supplemented by tradition and speculation. But the bookends - the opening praise to God and the final praise to the blessings left to us as a result of Jesus's ministry and mission - require no such movement, as these are eternal truths. And so the poem settles to pure celebration.

In all the verses it is best to imagine this as set to music, specifically Beethoven's 9th Symphony. This is how most people today first encountered this meter and rhyme scheme, whether in German (courtesy of Schiller) or in English through Christopher Wordsworth's "Hymn to Joy." And as with any song, the stressed syllables are more important than the others, allowing for some flexibility in the lines.

I, for one, found it very hard not to sing along (albeit to myself) as I read this.

Gary Mesick

ACKNOWLEDGMENTS

Joe and Katherine Galagan, husband and wife, are co-editors and have formatted this and all my prior published books. Katherine obtained her Doctor of Medicine degree from the University of Washington in Seattle, followed by a residency in Pathology at Upstate Medical Center in Syracuse, New York, finishing her residency at the University of Washington with a special emphasis in Hematopathology. Katherine has edited and co-authored several color atlases for the College of American Pathologists. Joe received a Bachelor of Arts degree in English Literature from the University of Washington, then a Masters' degree in Anglo/Irish Literature from University College in Dublin, Ireland, and finally, a Masters' degree in Counseling from Syracuse University in New York.

Gary Mesick received a Doctorate in English Literature from Harvard University. Before that he was a student at the U.S. Military Academy at West Point, graduating as an infantry officer. He returned to the Military Academy to teach English Literature to new cadets after receiving his doctorate. Gary has provided the Foreword for this book and also for several prior books, for which I am grateful.

Justin Connelly provided the cover art work. I have known his father Jack for years, and asked if he could recommend an artist for the front cover art work. He replied, "I know a fine artist, my son Justin." I could not more enthusiastically agree with Jack; Justin is a fine artist, and I appreciate his cover art work.

John Patrick McDonough (unrelated) is a poet, author,

and teacher of philosophy and theology at Mercyhurst Prep,, in Erie, Pennsylvania. We refer to each other as brothers in writing.

Finally, there is Bob McKamey and the music makers in the choir of St. Patrick Church and school in Tacoma. My first inkling to begin writing *Ode to Joy* may have started with his, and their rendition of "Hymn to Joy", repeated several times during the Easter season. Bob recently passed away, but his melodies still swirl about in my mind.

John R. McDonough

ODE TO JOY

JOHN R. MCDONOUGH

Prologue

I began writing this, wanting to portray the Holy Family from the perspective of a physician and father of seven children; and wanting to bring out the humanity in addition to the spiritual and blessed qualities of Mary Jesus and Joseph. Joy became the focus, and the ode became my writing style.

From early boyhood I was exposed to classical music, and developed a love for this, and for the great composers, but especially for the works of Beethoven. His Ninth Symphony became my favorite, especially the fourth movement with the voices. Then, in our parish church singing, especially during Easter season masses, we sang Christopher Wordsworth's "Hymn to Joy". The harmonics were those of Beethoven's Ninth Symphony. That is when I decided to incorporate this metric into my writing. Herein is Christopher Wordsworth's "Hymn to Joy", written in 1862:

Alleluia, Alleluia! Hearts to Heav'n and voices raise:
Sing to God a hymn of gladness, sing to God a hymn of praise.
Christ who on the cross as victim for the world's salvation died,
Jesus Christ, the King of glory, now is risen from the dead.

Now the iron bars are broken, Christ from death to life is born,
Glorious life, and life immortal, on this holy Easter morn.
Christ has triumphed, and we conquer by his mighty enterprise,
Jesus Christ, the King of glory, now is risen from the dead.

Christ is risen, we are risen, shed upon us heavenly grace,
Rain and dew and gleams of glory from your holy radiant face.
Then with hearts in heaven dwelling, we on earth your servants true,
Will by angel hands be gathered and be ever Lord with you.

1

Alleluia, Alleluia! Glory be to God on high,
Alleluia to the Savior, who has won the victory.
Alleluia to the Spirit, fount of life and sanctity,
Alleluia, Alleluia! to the Triune Majesty.

Wordsworth wrote his hymn based upon the metrics of Beethoven's Ninth Symphony, especially the fourth movement. Beethoven, on the other hand, was moved to write the Ninth Symphony (in 1824), inspired by the poem: "Ode to Joy", written in 1785, by Friedrich Schiller. The poem is written in German; I can only provide an English translation (by Michael Kay):

"An die Freude"
by Friedrich Schiller

Joy! A spark of fire from heaven,
Daughter from Elysium,
Drunk with fire we dare to enter,
Holy one inside your shrine.
Your magic power binds together,
What we by custom wrench apart,
All men will emerge as brothers,
Where we rest your gentle wings.

If you've mastered that great challenge:
Giving friendship to a friend,
If you've earned a steadfast woman,
Celebrate your joy with us!
Join if in the whole wide world there's
Just one soul to call your own!
He who's failed must steal away,
Shedding tears as he departs.

All creation drinks with pleasure,
Drinks at Mother Nature's breast,
All the just, and all the evil,
Follow down her rosy path.
Kisses she bestowed, and grape wine,
Friendship true, proved e'en in death,
Every worm knows nature's pleasure,
Every cherub meets his God.

Gladly, like the planets flying
True to heaven's mighty plan,
Brothers, run your course now,
Happy as a knight in victory.

Be embraced, all you millions,
Share this kiss with all the world!
Way above the stars, brothers,
There must live a loving father.
Do you kneel down low, you millions?
Do you see your maker, world?
Search for Him above the stars,
Above the stars he must be living.

And there's more. In 1907, American Henry Van Dyke wrote this poem while staying at the home of Williams College President Harry Augustus Garfield. This version is beloved in Protestant churches throughout the United States:

Joyful, joyful, we adore Thee
God of glory, Lord of love,
Hearts unfold like flow'rs before Thee
Op'ning to the Sun above.
Melt the clouds of sin and sadness

drive the dark of doubt away,
Giver of immortal gladness
fill us with the light of day.

All Thy works with joy surround Thee
Earth and heav'n reflect Thy rays,
Stars and angels sing around Thee
center of unbroken praise.
Field and forest, vale and mountain
Flow'ry meadow, flashing sea,
chanting bird and flowing fountain
call us to rejoice in Thee.

Thou art giving and forgiving
ever blessing, ever blest,
well-spring of the joy of living
ocean-depth of happy rest.
Thou the Father, Christ our Brother—
all who live in love are Thine.
Teach us how to love each other
lift us to the Joy Divine.

Mortals join the mighty chorus
which the morning stars began,
Father-love is reigning o'er us
brother-love binds man to man.
Ever singing, march we onward
victors in the midst of strife.
joyful music lifts us sunward
in the triumph song of life.

In 1972 the Council of Europe adopted Beethoven's "Ode to Joy" theme as its anthem. Then in 1985, it was adopted as the official anthem of the European Union, which includes the music without words.

4

Canto 1: God with Us

A TRIUNE GOD

God in heaven God is sovereign
  God our sovereign meant to be
First forever God creator
  Heaven there eternally

God creator God forever
  God in heaven meant to be
First and foremost ever after
  Heaven based eternally

Our creator three in person
  Father Son and Spirit be
Bountiful is God's creation
  We do see and we agree

God in heaven God universal
  God transcendent evermore
Beauty goodness truth forever
  Love entwining we adore

MARY, THE IMMACULATE CONCEPTION

Original sin from our first parents
  Clearly disobeying God
Carried to all future humans
  Death then added not so odd

God in his deliberation
  Love and mercy in full sway
Sought the means for our salvation
  Only God could be the way

God to enter human nature
  And God's mother to be pure
Removal of all sin required
  Needed to provide the cure

At the proper time selected
  God chose Anne and Joachim
Parents of then sinless Mary
  To be mother to bear him

GOD BE WITH US

Jewish mid-teen girl a virgin
  Mary lived a holy life
God prepared from time eternal
  For his mother free from strife

God eternal God forever
  Chose his Mary ever blessed
God in heaven chose this woman
  One of us that he caressed

God sent Gabriel archangel
  To tell Mary on that day
She to bear and be a mother
  What oh Mary dost thou say

How can this be I know not man
  God's own Spirit will do this
I accept as thou hast stated
  Pregnant now with God's own kiss

MARY VISITS ELIZABETH

Angel Gabriel told Mary
  At the Annunciation
That her cousin Elizabeth
  Was six months pregnant with a son

Elizabeth at advanced age
  Well beyond conceiving time
Mary and Joseph left to visit
  Elizabeth a trip sublime

Upon hearing Mary's greeting
  Babe in her womb leapt with joy
Blessed art thou among women
  And the fruit of thy womb a boy

Mary stayed for three months to help
  Elizabeth's delivery
Mary thus became a midwife
  Part of Mary's history

THE DREAM

Joseph married to wife Mary
  Both to each remaining chaste
Oath to God and to each other
  Adoration they both graced

Nazareth was home for Joseph
  From Jerusalem they went
Carpentry to earn a living
  Shared with poor their income spent

Days then weeks elapsed together
  Then a problem Mary's bulge
Silently should he divorce her
  Publicly then not divulge

Joseph in a dream was given
  From an angel to fear naught
Infant to be king messiah
  By the Holy Spirit brought

THE NATIVITY

Called to venture where they came from
  By Augustus' famed decree
Searching searching yet no room for
  Crowds have taken all to be

Hurry Joseph pangs have started
  Hurry please no time to wait
Then the birth cave opened for them
  Scattered straw was Mary's fate

Angel duo in the foreground
  When enclosing waters broke
Head was crowning then was outside
  Into waiting angel's stroke

Next the shoulder with a slight turn
  Entered into candle light
First the baby then placenta
  Placed on straw to lay in sight

THE AFTERBIRTH

Placenta used to auto-transfuse
  Blood to newborn on the straw
Gently stroked until no more through
  Ligate cord and then withdraw

Hold head down to drain the water
  Torso tapped to be the link
Infant breathing regularly
  Skin was blue now turning pink

Angels took good care of baby
  Gently placed near Mary's arm
Placenta then removed by angels
  All to keep from doing harm

Baby now moved up to Mary
  Softly placed against her breast
Milk now flowing baby feeding
  Both now wonderfully blessed

THE SHEPHERDS

Angels sang and shepherds listened
  Newborn king of Israel
In a manger off and yonder
  Lying in a manger still

Shepherds came and cave was entered
  Manger filled with straw so bright
Now it held a newborn baby
  Radiating heaven's light

Mother Mary sitting resting
  Near her baby's manger side
Next to her was Joseph standing
  Watching waiting time to bide

Cows and sheep were in the manger
  Breathing heat on this cold night
Silence now was dominating
  Joy and peace now their delight

THE CIRCUMCISION

Other lodging found for family
  Baby fed from mother's breast
Week went by then to the Temple
  Circumcision to attest

By what name for this male infant
  Asked the Temple priest on site
His name Jesus angel given
  Parents gave as their delight

Obsidian knife blade was then handed
  Sharper than a scalpel's steel
Foreskin deftly held and severed
  Remnant soothed with balm to heal

Eight days birth to circumcision
  Covenant to man applied
Male infant's flesh is taken
  Jesus man and God complied

THE WISE MEN

Wise men came from Persia guided
  By a star that drew them west
Caspar Melchior Balthazar and
  With companions on their quest

Knowing Scripture and the heavens
  Newborn king of Israel
Bethlehem with star to guide them
  Journey theirs as was their call

Gold and myrrh and frankincense came
  Gifts of worship for their king
Finding Jesus Mary Joseph
  With their presence gifts to bring

In a dream the angel told them
  Take a different route than shown
Herod jealous will harm infant
  Killing him to keep his throne

FLEE TO EGYPT

Joseph in a dream was told to
  Flee to Egypt no delay
Angel said that Herod threatened*
  Go now from this do not stray

Stay in Egypt till I tell you
  To return from where you were
Dead of night and holy family
  Left the birthplace to transfer

On through Gaza City* they passed
  South through leagues of desert vast
Mary Jesus astride donkey
  Joseph leading all steadfast

Heliopolis in Egypt
  Destined to be journey's end
Jesus grew to be a young boy
  Seven years was theirs to spend

*I wrote these words on May 18th, 2024, during the Israeli-Hamas war. A parallel exists between Herod's ordering the death of male infants 2 years and younger (the holy innocents), and a modern-day Herod (Benjamin Netanyahu), ordering the aerial bombing of Gaza, resulting in the mass killing of innocent Palestinian children.

Canto 2: The Early Years

GOD WITH US

Heliopolis (modern Cairo)
  Was the holy family's joy
Seven years was Jesus growing
  Suckling to a strong young boy

What of things that many families
  Run into as children grow
Squabbles illness temper tantrums
  Weaning diapers all in tow

We don't know can only wonder
  Of the holy family's deeds
Jesus growing needed parents
  To provide his body's needs

King Messiah God and Sonship
  These were for a future time
They must now see being human
  Carries with it dirt and grime

EARLY TRAINING

Carpentry was Joseph's trade then
 Jesus from the age of six
Was taught different kinds of lumber
 And the varied tools to fix

Early Jesus taught to bring things
 To the bench for Joseph's work
Then to clean the bench of shavings
 His to clean and not to shirk

Later after fetch and clean up
 Use of tools was then shown
Measure twice then saw remember
 Keeps you from a forlorn groan

Another year of helping Joseph
 Gaining skills in family's shed
In a dream the angel stated
 Leave now Joseph Herod's dead

LEAVING HELIOPOLIS

While in Egypt seven years there
  Neighbor friends were theirs to know
Bonds of friendship and attachment
  Virtue goodness theirs to show

Jesus surely had his neighbor's
  Other children his own age
Did they play the games of children
  How did Jesus thus engage

Virtue goodness from young Jesus
  To his playmates would impress
They then felt God's grace within them
  Wondrous closeness to possess

Joseph Mary packed the donkey
  For the trek to their homestead
Nazareth their destination
  Their long journey far ahead

NAZARETH EARLY YEARS

Desert travel with the donkey
  Walk or ride the leagues each day
Mary riding on the donkey
  Joseph Jesus steps away

At long last they reached their homestead
  Nazareth now theirs to stay
Carpentry still Joseph's trade work
  Home keeping was Mary's way

Worship at the nearby temple
  Three times yearly theirs ahead
Some feasts could be for the family
  Others were for men instead

This was quiet time for family
  Jesus grew to age of twelve
Helping Joseph with his wood work
  Fetching tools from off the shelf

UNLEAVENED BREAD

Holy family to the temple
  Feast of the Unleavened Bread
On returning to their home site
  Jesus was not at their stead

Hurry Joseph we must go back
  Search for Jesus on the way
He was in the temple teaching
  Elders priests that very day

Mary asked why have you done this
  Causing us to worry so
I must be about my Father's
  Work do woman you not know

Much to ponder in Passover
  Unleavened bread and bloodied posts
Crucifixion's crown and nails
  And the Eucharistic hosts

THE QUIET YEARS

Returning from Jerusalem's holy
  Temple wherein Jesus taught
Priests and rabbis were amazed at
  Insights the boy Jesus brought

Months and years then for the family
  Hidden from the scripture's view
Living growing time elapsing
  Like the lives we all pass through

This was time of preparation
  For the start of public life
Jesus grew from boy to manhood
  Happy times devoid of strife

Ordinary things that families
  Each and every day need done
Working cleaning dumping garbage
  Jesus surely would not shun

DEATH OF JOSEPH

Joseph reached the age of sixty*
  When his health began to fail
Jesus then took up the burden
  Family order to prevail

Mary Jesus turned to Joseph
  Seeing to his every need
Feeding bathing and providing
  Comfort for his every heed

Slowly weakness then prevailed
  Bedrest needed through the day
Family saw that death approaching
  Calm and peace were their display

Death then came to holy Joseph
  Held in family's close embrace
Death for us should not be final
  Rather change to heaven's place

*Venerable Mary of Jesus Agreda, *The Mystical City of God (1670)*, Abridgment, TAN Books, Saint Bernard Press, LLC, Charlotte, North Carolina, 1978, p. 316

Canto 3: Public Life

BAPTISM OF JESUS

Leaving Mary at their homestead
  Jesus left for Bethany
John baptizing in the Jordan
  Crowds had formed there handily

Approaching Jesus stood in line there
  John then felt an inner glow
Baptize me John said to Jesus
  This for me to undergo

Jesus answered no I'm here for
  You to baptize me here and now
John complied with Jesus' asking
  John the Baptist did allow

Standing in the Jordan River
  Water poured when Baptist done
Dove appeared and Father uttered
  This is my beloved Son

PUBLIC LIFE

Leaving Nazareth Jesus started
  Journeying his public stance
Mary was with him as always
  Helping him at every chance

Men he met stood up to follow
  Women too joined with the crowd
Twelve began later apostles
  More disciples then allowed

Jesus and his followers moved from
  Place to place and town to town
Teaching curing and example
  Kingdom thus on solid ground

How could this small entourage be
  Of the future kingdom come
Surely God must be behind this
  Fashioned from this tiny crumb

MARRIAGE FEAST AT CANA

Invited friends and family
　Were Mary Jesus and his friends
To a marriage feast of plenty
　Cana near where Nazareth ends

Bride and groom and large entourage
　Gathered for the marriage rites
Celebrating started early
　Food and drink were their delights

Groom's attendant came to Mary
　Saying there is no more wine
Hearing Jesus said to Mary
　But my time is not yet thine

Fill these stone jugs full of water
　Attendant said these are fine wines
Best for last is not the usual
　First of Jesus' many signs

KINGDOM OF GOD

What do lamps and mustard seeds and
  Pearls leaven and a net
Have in common these are odd things
  Yet we have them in our debt

Used by Jesus to connect us
  To God's kingdom yet so near
Odd disparate things around us
  Used to make his teaching clear

Lighted lamp not meant to be placed
  Under bushel basket lid
Pearl of great price acquire it
  Net to capture fish and squid

What of mustard seed so tiny
  Sown becomes a full-sized tree
Branches used by birds to nest in
  Dough with leaven bread to be

AVOIDING SCANDAL

Woe to the world because of scandal
  Said Jesus to the apostles
Who receives the littlest ones
  Becomes mine in the gospels

Who then causes the least to sin
  Were better for him to foresee
A millstone wrapped around his neck
  And be drowned in depths of sea

Woe to the world when scandals fare
  And to men whom scandals stem
Best to cut off thy hand or foot
  And to separate thee from them

If eye an occasion for sin
  Pluck it out and cast it away
Best to be maimed or lamed in life
  Than eternal hell's fire stay

DANGER OF RICHES

Rich man rich man be aware of
  Peril riches hold for thee
Euro dollar or some other
  All effect in some degree

Rich young man encountered Jesus
  Master what more can I do
I have kept all ten commandments
  Gave to the poor what is their due

Else the rich remain contorted
  Miserly unto their stealth
Death then brings eternal misery
  Money steals from heaven's wealth

What will bring eternal glory
  Formula is alms and tithe
For the poor and church the story
  Thence the rich are free and lithe

CURING THE BLIND

Leaving Jericho behind then
 Jesus bound for Jerusalem
Followers and crowds came after
 Two blind men were there with them

Hearing Jesus passing nearby
 Hollered Jesus son of David
Crowds then tried to silence them
 Mercy on us blind men stated

Jesus stopped and calling them said
 What would you have me to do
Lord that our eyes could be opened
 This is what we want from you

Jesus with compassion reached and
 Touched the eyes of both blind men
Instantly they regained eyesight
 Followed Jesus saw again

RAISING LAZARUS

Bethany was home to Mary
  Martha and to Lazarus
Lazarus is sick Lord Jesus
  Brother to the two of us

Hearing this from sister Mary
  Jesus stayed for two more days
Then proceeded to Judea
  Delay used to suit his ways

Lazarus is dead said Jesus
  To those following his stead
He is in the tomb four days now
  Mary stated well ahead

Take away the stone said Jesus
  Lazarus come out from there
Wrapped in cloth came Lazarus walking
  Healthy and without a care

AUTHORITY OF JESUS

Jesus by whose authority
  Do you teach and cure the sick
Questioned the chief priests and elders
  Implying his some kind of a trick

Jesus had cured on the sabbath
  A man lame for thirty-eight years
According to these same chief priests
  A sacrilege done it appears

Jesus gave answer as follows
  Amen amen I say to you
The son can do nothing himself
  Only what the father can do

You cannot honor the father
  If you do not honor the son
The son has the power to judge
  The son and the father are one

THE GREATEST COMMANDMENT

The scribe asked Jesus which is first
  The greatest commandment of all
The first commandment of all is
  Love thy God that is the call

With thy whole heart thy whole soul
  With thy whole strength and whole mind
This is the first and my command
  Love God as herein defined

The second commandment of love
  Love thy neighbor as thyself
No other commandment is greater
  Remember keep love on your shelf

Now let us go on a bit more
  Neighbor should mean everyone
Even those who do you wrong
  Forgive them all for what was done

BEATITUDE AND WOE

Blessed are the poor in spirit
  Woe the rich and powerful
Blessed are those who now hunger
  Woe the rich and comfortable

Blessed those at times who mourn
  Woe to you who laugh forlorn
Blessed are the meek and humble
  Woe to those who meekness scorn

Blessed are the merciful
  Woe the rich who ply their force
Mercy given love begotten
  Woe those using wrath their source

Blessed are the clean of heart
  Woe those chastity deny
Blessed are the peacemakers
  Woe those who do not apply

TRANSFIGURATION

Oh to turn the clock back on then
  Add some years be young again
Yet we know that we cannot but
  Capture time with ink and pen

Jesus did this very same thing
  Mountain trip with John and James
His visage then shone as bright sun
  Others came with different names

Moses and Elias entered
  Both conversed with James and John
Ordinary conversation
  Both yet from a time long gone

What must be the power then wielded
  Making time turn on itself
God's own power must have caused this
  Man could not from his own self

STORM AT SEA

This was not a liner or great ship
  Rather small and made of wood
Disciples inside were the crew
  While Jesus slept aft for their good

A storm arose upon the sea
  Great waves then washed over the boat
Save us Lord we are perishing
  Jesus awake and heard their quote

Why fearful you of little faith
  He stood rebuking sea and wind
A sudden calm the boat sailed free
  His the power to rescind

The men aboard those caught in fear
  Said what manner of man is this
Even the wind and sea obey
  Now saved from the prior abyss

WALKING ON WATER

Jesus went to the mount to pray
  Disciples on boat out at sea
It was night and the boat was buffeted
  Jesus be with us their plea

Then Jesus came walking toward them
  Walking on water which they saw
It's a ghost they cried out in fear
  Wishing that they could withdraw

Then Jesus spoke to them these words
  It is I take courage no fear
Peter asked let me come to you
  Come Peter said Jesus near

Peter walked then started to sink
  The men in the boat were awed
Rescued by Jesus they all stated
  Truly thou art the son of God

JESUS PREDICTS HIS PASSION

Jesus on his travels with the twelve
Took them aside and said to them
We go to Jerusalem where
  Chief priests and elders will condemn

The son of man will be betrayed
To be abused and mocked and scourged
Delivered to the gentiles where
  The sins of men will thus be purged

He will then be crucified
  After being condemned to death
He will hang upon the cross
  Until taking his last breath

He will then be taken down
  And be buried in the tomb
Yet on the third day he will rise
  And be seen in the upper room

TRIUMPHAL ENTRY

This the feast of unleavened bread
  Passover was meant to them
Jesus with his disciples
  Journeyed to Jerusalem

Crowds that gathered sought out Jesus
  Regarding him a messiah
Cutting branches from the palm trees
  For Jesus this was their gala

Jesus said go to the village
  Bring to me colt of an ass
If they ask why do you take this
  Answer master's need alas

They placed cloaks upon the road
  Blessed is he who comes as king
Glory to the name of the Lord
  Peace to heaven they did sing

LAST SUPPER

This is my body this my blood
  Said Jesus in the upper room
With bread in hand and cup of wine
  And killed next day then to the tomb

He must be mad a lunatic
  Thought one outside on hearing this
While twelve inside accepted him
  His followers would not dismiss

This happened on a Thursday night
  With Jesus Mary and the twelve
But we might wonder lunacy
  If there was nothing more to delve

Believe and follow otherwise
  There is no space to straddle
His utterance is God's own word
  Not lowly human prattle

BETRAYAL

One of you will betray me soon
  Said Jesus to his gathered twelve
He who dips his hand in the dish
  With mine will be the one himself

Better that he never was born
  Then Judas asked is it I Lord
Jesus answered thou has said it
  Then Judas left for his reward

Thirty pieces of silver paid
  To Judas for his treachery
The one that I kiss will be he
  Capture him immediately

Judas keeper of the purse
  But he became a chronic thief
An all-consuming greed was his
  Foreshadowing eternal grief

PETER'S DENIAL

During the last supper meal
  Holy communion was for twelve
Jesus with eleven now
  Judas gone for them to delve

Jesus then to eleven said
  This night you will be scandalized
I the shepherd will be stricken
  Sheep then scattered vandalized

Peter answered I will never
  Be scandalized because of thee
Before the cock crows Jesus answered
  Thrice this night you will deny me

Peter answered back and then said
  I will die but not deny
Others there said same as Peter
  Time will tell if these apply

Canto 4: Passion and Death

AGONY IN THE GARDEN

Moving to the mount of olives
  With disciples on the way
He took Peter James and John
  To the garden and to pray

Jesus prayed then to his father
  Saddened trembling there as one
Let this cup pass away from me
  Yet thy will not mine be done

A cold sweat as drops of blood came
  Running down upon the ground
Heaven's angel then appeared to
  Strengthen him as duty bound

Could you not stay awake and pray
  Jesus told the sleeping three
But they began to sleep again
  Despite his sorrow and his plea

JESUS ARRESTED

Jesus left with his disciples
  The last supper then allowed
It was night and in the torchlight
  Judas came with a large crowd

Bearing swords and clubs they caught him
  Judas leading with a kiss
Peter drew his sword and cut off
  A servant's ear without a miss

Put thy sword back then said Jesus
  Those that use will perish by it
If I entreat my father now
  Twelve legions angels he will fit

To the crowd Jesus admonished
  You have come as for a robber
I sat daily with you teaching
  Now you've come to me to clobber

JESUS BEFORE THE SANHEDRIN

Caiaphas high priest and elders
  Sat as court confronting Jesus
He does not answer our demands
  Standing silent to displease us

By the living God adjure thee
  Art thou Christ the son of God
Jesus answered thou has said it
  Blasphemy this does seem odd

Caiaphas then tore his garments
  We will need no further witness
They in unison then answered
  Death for him will be our business

They then slapped and spat upon him
  But not on the sabbath day
Could they go and crucify him
  They then found another way

JESUS BEFORE PILATE

Pontius Pilate Procurator
　Was the next to question him
Art thou then the king of the jews
　Thou sayest it said Jesus grim

Pilate knew the jews had brought him
　Out of envy to so thrust
Pilate's wife a fitful dream said
　Do no harm this man is just

Pilate found no laws were broken
　Jesus thus was innocent
Jesus or Barabbas Pilate
　Said one released munificent

We want Jesus crucify him
　Screamed the crowd incited by the jews
Send Barabbas then back to us
　We want Jesus to abuse

THE END OF JUDAS

Better that he never was born
  Words by Jesus meant for Judas
Shortly after his betrayal
  Act when taken not delude us

He repented to the chief priests
  I have betrayed innocent blood
The thirty pieces of silver
  He flung on the floor as a flood

But what is it to us they said
  Take care of it thyself
We now have our work to do
  Go and leave it to ourself

Shaken craven Judas left them
  Searched for then what he could see
Finding bridle rope he then used
  Hanging himself upon a tree

JESUS SCOURGED

Roman scourging terrible beating
  Stripped then tied to post of stone
Flagellum the tool of torment
  Oxen hide with shards and bone

Thus was Jesus tied and pummeled
  Roman soldiers on each side
Taking turns they flagellated
  Strips of skin that opened wide

Blood that splattered on to others
  And seeped down onto the ground
Soldiers out to hit the hardest
  Jesus making not a sound

Roman leader there was watchful
  Lest the scourge be cause of death
Back all bloody Jesus sagging
  And becoming short of breath

JESUS CROWNED WITH THORNS

Soldiers knowing Jesus' claim
 That he was the son of God
Made a stout branch full of thorns
 This a crown his head has clawed

Then they placed a scarlet robe
 On his bloodied shoulders bare
Next a reed placed in his hand
 They then knelt in mock fanfare

Hail king of the jews they chimed
 While spitting upon his face
Taking the reed from out his hand
 They pounded his head apace

Thorns were sharp and penetrated
 Through his scalp and to the bone
 Causing pain so agonizing
 His to bear our sins atone

JESUS CARRIES HIS CROSS

They then removed the royal robe
  And replaced his own vesture
Selecting one Simon Cyrene
  Helping with their next gesture

Simon was then forced to carry
  This burden a cross of wood
Shoulder to shoulder with Jesus
  Lifting the heavy cross they stood

Crowds lamenting on the journey
  Women of Jerusalem weep
For yourselves and your children
  They proceeded at a creep

Jesus fell along the way
  Then Veronica wiped his face
An image appearing on the cloth
  A perfect replica in its place

THE CRUCIFIXION

Jesus carried Simon bore
 The cross piece on their shoulders sore
To Golgotha place of the skull
 Dragged there half a mile or more

The cross was placed flat on the ground
 Jesus stripped placed on the cross
His body braced on the long member
 His arms were stretched firmly across

Nails pounded through his palms
 Then between bones of his feet
The cross was then raised straight upright
 The soldiers' efforts now complete

There was a sign nailed at the top
 In latin greek and in hebrew
This is Jesus king of the jews
 Reflecting what those soldiers knew

THE ROBBERS

Two robbers one on either side
  With Jesus were then crucified
If thou art the Christ then save us
  And thyself this robber sighed

The other in answer rebuked
  We receive what we deserve
But this man has done nothing wrong
  Do you not fear God and observe

Lord coming into thy kingdom
  Remember me all that I've said
Two thieves and the Lord crucified
  Awaiting what just lay ahead

Jesus turning aside his head
  To the good thief had this to say
Amen amen thou shalt be
  In paradise with me this day

THREE HOURS ON THE CROSS

Many words were spoken that day
  By Jesus aloft and on the cross
To the good thief paradise said
  To the crowd I thirst his loss

To his father forgive them
  For they know not what they do
To Mary woman behold thy son
  John this is your mother too

Hanging there was heard to say
  My God my God why hast thou
Crowds heard this and then what followed
  Forsaken me right here and now

It is finished father into
  Thy hands I commend my spirit
For the thieves their legs were broken
  Jesus dead and incoherent

THE LANCE

Jesus dead upon the cross
  Three long hours hanging there
The two thieves with broken legs
  Were taken down a grim affair

Then a soldier Longinus
  Came forward with a lance
To pierce the side of Jesus
  To ensure a macabre dance

Trained in battle Longinus
  Desired to pierce Jesus' heart
But Jesus was high upon the cross
  The concern was where to start

Longinus knew from his training
  To strike from below the rib cage
The right atrium then was entered
  The blood and serum oozing stage

THE AFTERMATH

When Jesus died the sky became
  Dark at midday and the curtain
Of the temple torn asunder
  Many doubting then felt certain

The centurion moved with wonder
  Said truly this was a just man
Women weeping in the background
  Were with crowds since this began

Good man Joseph councillor asked
  Pilate for the burial rite
Jesus body was then taken
  Buried the tomb out of sight

Jewish priests and pharisees then
  Went to Pilate for a guard
Saying three days he would rise
  Use yours said Pilate in regard

Canto 5: Resurrection and Ascension

THE RESURRECTION

Two Mary's one was Magdalen
  Came and found the stone rolled back
Do not fear an angel said
  Jesus is risen now make track

Tell his disciples he is risen
  Behold to Galilee he goes
Quickly they departed knowing
  They should say as the angel chose

Then two left running for the tomb
  Peter running slower than John
John waited then Peter went in
  Empty head cloth folded on

John came next and was astounded
  The empty tomb had this effect
Both disciples then remembered
  Jesus predicted this direct

POSTING OF THE GUARDS

Priests and pharisees had posted
  Guards around the tomb to stay
Then when Jesus rose that morning
  They were terrified that day

Guards then went back to the city
  Telling priests what they had seen
They had felt an earthquake shaking
  Then an angel on the scene

They lay on the ground and trembled
  Pretending that they were dead
Priests and pharisees then huddled
  Figuring out what should be said

Money given and guards told to
  Say his disciples came by night
Stole him away while we were sleeping
  We will protect you as our right

MARY MAGDALEN AT THE TOMB

Mary Magdalen stood weeping
  Near the tomb hewn out of rock
This where she had taken spices
  To anoint after her walk

Back at the tomb now empty
  She had not yet seen the Lord
Then she saw this man the gardener
  Who could not but be ignored

Woman why art thou now weeping
  Woman whom dost thou now seek
Sir if thou hast removed him
  I will take him hear my pique

Jesus turned and said Mary
  Mary beaming said teacher
Jesus living and breathing
  Extended his hand to reach her

THE ROAD TO EMMAUS

Walking the road to Emmaus
  The two men discussed as they strode
Events that each had witnessed
  What his death and burial told

As they walked a stranger joined them
  Asking why you seem so sad
What now are you talking about
  Is there anything I can add

Do you not know the predictions
  The Christ had to suffer and die
They stopped and asked stay with us
  Time to eat but we need your reply

At table the stranger took bread
  He blessed it and gave to the two
Their eyes were then opened to see
  T'was Jesus they were speaking to

THE UPPER ROOM

His twelve now eleven were stunned
In the upper room waiting there
Jesus then stood in their midst
They panicked as if not aware

Peace to you be not afraid
But thinking they had seen a ghost
Then Jesus said I am here
And seeing him they were engrossed

See and feel me and see my wounds
Do you have anything to eat
They brought honeycomb and fish
With relish he devoured this treat

When satisfied some food was left
He gave to them what then remained
He taught as scriptures this God's plan
Leaving when this was ingrained

DOUBTING THOMAS

Thomas was not there when Jesus came
  Others said we have seen the Lord
Unless I see the nail marks
  I will not be of one accord

One week hence with Thomas there
  The upper room as was before
The doors were closed but Jesus came
  Showing himself to them once more

Incredulous was Thomas now
  Seeing Jesus with his eyes
Peace be to you Jesus said
  Place your hands and be thou wise

Thomas answered my Lord and God
  Jesus then said blessed are they
Who have not seen and yet believed
  Jesus then disappeared away

THOSE FORTY DAYS

After resurrecting from the dead
  Jesus stayed for forty more days
Seen by people in Jerusalem
  Hundreds maybe thousands to amaze

As a doctor I would want to know
  The status of his wounds back then
Hands and feet his side and head
  Are they oozing blood again

Yet when Thomas first saw Jesus
  Only two weeks from the dead
Bring forth thy finger to my hand
  Thy hand into my side Jesus said

Others surely flabbergasted
  Seeing Jesus walk with breath
Having seen his crucifixion
  Now arisen from his death

PRIMACY OF PETER

Thou art Peter upon this rock
  I will build my church Jesus said
The gates of hell will not prevail
  Against her triumphantly spread

Peter son of John do you love me
  Peter answered Lord you know I do
Then feed my lambs this a command
  This is what I want of you

Amen amen I say to thee
  When young thou didst gird thyself
When old thou wilt stretch forth thy hands
  Another will gird thee himself

Then lead thee to where thou wouldst not
  Signifying the road to death
Follow me Jesus then said to him
  I am with you through your last breath

COMMISSION OF THE APOSTLES

After resurrecting Jesus said
To his apostles being there
Await me in Jerusalem
There's more for you to be aware

Jesus approached and spoke to them
All power in heaven and on earth
Has been given to me go therefore
And make disciples a new birth

Baptizing them in the name
Of the Father and of the Son
And of the Holy Spirit
Three persons God as Triune one

Repentance and remission
Of all sins preached in my name
Make disciples in all nations
This is for you to proclaim

THE ASCENSION

After arising from the dead
 Jesus spent those forty days
Instructing his disciples
 About the kingdom and God's ways

Stay in Jerusalem and wait
 The Holy Spirit will come
And baptize you with his spirit
 Then apostles you become

Imagine how incredulous
 Those who saw and with him ate
Before hundreds maybe thousands
 He stood surrounded by their weight

Then slowly he began his ascent
 Slowly rising in the sky
A stark defying gravity
 Then disappearing up on high

Canto 6: Pentecost

COMING OF THE HOLY SPIRIT

Pentecost the fiftieth day
  After jewish Savuot
Celebrating passover
  The bringing of God's truth about

The upper room with the eleven
  And Mary Jesus' mother
A violent wind came howling as
  They stared at one another

Parted tongues like fire came
  And settled upon each
Then with the Holy Spirit filled
  Others they began to teach

Devout jews from every nation
  Also heard the violent wind
Then spoke in tongues all heard as one
  They therein were as of one mind

PETER'S WORDS

Peter stood with the eleven
  Men of Israel hear these words
Jesus of Nazareth was a man
  Approved by God through his concerns

Wonders miracles and signs
  In your midst as you all know
You have crucified and slain
  But God has raised him up to show

For David said I saw the Lord
  Because he is at my right hand
This is why my heart makes merry
  And for you to understand

Therefore let all Israel
  Most assuredly be aware
That God has made this Jesus Christ
  Lord for all this is my prayer

REPENT AND BE BAPTIZED

They asked Peter what shall we do
Repent and then be baptized
All in the name of Jesus Christ
This for you will be advised

For the forgiveness of your sins
And the Holy Spirit's gifts
For your children and those far off
Guilt of sin baptism lifts

Then the eleven apostles
In the name of the Father
The Son and the Holy Spirit
Began baptizing them as proper

The crowds came forth to be baptized
Three thousand underwent that day
Has there ever been such faith seen
Pentecost showed such grand array

Canto 7: Gifts of the Holy Spirit

GIFTS OF THE HOLY SPIRIT - WISDOM

The quality of being wise
  That accumulates with age
But only with the Spirit's grace
  For which lifelong we must engage

Experience to sort things out
  Especially after an overt act
To separate the right from wrong
  To provide a future track

To provide good judgement for
  Conflicting things that come to pass
Keeping goodness at the fore
  So evil thoughts do not surpass

It is the soundness of decision
  Of knowing when and what to do
Self directing one's behavior
  Retaining God's assistance through

GIFTS OF THE HOLY SPIRIT - KNOWLEDGE

Where should we look for knowledge
  To the tree of good and evil
Knowledge of good and evil
  Adam and Eve's upheaval

Puzzling that we start here
  That God did enjoin not to eat
The fruit an apple of that tree
  This an enigma how to treat

God could not mean knowledge alone
  Rather behavior that came
Actions leading us to sin
  Knowledge alone not be the blame

Knowledge should thus be sought after
  And treasured for its own sake
The Holy Spirit has given
  His blessing thus make no mistake

Like knowledge and yet not the same
  Understanding is felt deeper
A grasp of the connections
  Our mind's most dearest keeper

Understanding is to know
  The gift of ideation
Mindfulness a part of soul
  Eternal God's creation

And yet to know of only things
  Is not its major function
To know of God the Trinity
  And our association

Is deep set in our mindfulness
  The Holy Spirit's gift to us
Removes us from the transient
  Forever made our mind says thus

GIFTS OF THE HOLY SPIRIT - COUNSEL

Counsel means to give or seek advice
  The Holy Spirit thus begins
To counsel as our lives unfold
  Especially to forgive our sins

Lead us not into temptation
  But deliver us from evil
These last lines from our Lord's prayer
  Puts the focus on retrieval

The sacrament of Penance
  Or reconciliation
Provides remission of our sins
  Our church's obligation

Enter the confessional
  And to the priest confess our sins
Absolution sins forgiven
  Peace and joy new life begins

GIFTS OF THE HOLY SPIRIT - FORTITUDE

Surely valor on the battle field
  Bravery in the threat of danger
What of other hidden efforts
  When the other is a stranger

But the Spirit's gift goes farther
  Grace when things go far awry
Especially when evil threatens
  And goodness seems in short supply

What of single mothers' struggles
  To provide for children's needs
And those poor who work two jobs
  Lest dissolution supersedes

Surely maintenance of virtue
  When temptation's threats apply
Fortitude for holy measures
  Prayer then should be our reply

GIFTS OF THE HOLY SPIRIT - PIETY

Reverence the Spirit's gift
  Devotion to the sacraments
And to the church which God did give
  And to the church's documents

Those documents encompass wide
  Those teachings brought to earth
By Jesus when he lived with us
  Beyond his incarnate birth

Follow me his ardent word
  To Peter and the apostles
Encompassed in those noble works
  New testament the gospels

And meaning also for those souls
  In search of deeper peace
Mass and eucharistic food
  Fosters holiness to increase

Why fear when it is God we love
  And he said do not be afraid
Then change the word from fear to love
  Becoming then a worthy trade

The meaning should be revered awe
  To honor his great glory
This will make much better sense
  And add to God's own story

We also need to please the Lord
  Doing nothing to offend him
Leading lives of holiness
  Making this our daily hymn

We should not with a worried fear
  Be how we should then relish God
Let love and reverence be our all
  Instead of fear's fearsome facade

Canto 8: Fruits of the Holy Spirit

FRUITS OF THE HOLY SPIRIT - CHARITY

Charity should begin at home
  An adage of long standing
And one of double meaning
  Conflicting understanding

One meaning speaks of money
  That family needs come first
Only then should other use
  For funds to be dispersed

Another meaning is of love
  God first then self as neighbor
Jesus gave us this command
  Making this our utmost labor

Combine the two and find they meld
  Use alms and tithes to alter
The plight of neighbors near and far
  Love placed upon God's altar

FRUITS OF THE HOLY SPIRIT - JOY

Joy is felt a deep contentment
  Not a temporary thing
Like a transient satisfaction
  Such as eaten meals bring

Joy is based upon conviction
  Faith in God with truth and good
Living life unto its fullest
  Vagaries are understood

Pleasures leading to sinfulness
  Leave a wanton empty dross
Warping goodness that is in us
  Feelings of a terrible loss

There are those holy sacraments
  Baptism confirmation
Penance and the eucharist
  Bring joy in application

FRUITS OF THE HOLY SPIRIT - PEACE

Peace like joy a deep contentment
  Comfort from within the soul
And with turmoil all around us
  Lets us keep within control

War and peace our history shows us
  War is waged goes on and on
We are victims of its ravage
  Persons thus are put upon

But the inner peace bespoken
  Does not harbor sad despair
Even when the world is darkness
  Keep the grace of peace to share

Inner peace a gift of God's grace
  Overwhelms both pain and death
Early christian martyrs showed us
  Peaceful hymns to their last breath

FRUITS OF THE HOLY SPIRIT - PATIENCE

Tolerance of troubles come what may
  Equipoise while being on a limb
Endurance without anger thus
  Putting up without a furtive whim

Patience is foundational to be
  Strong when varied difficulties mount
Hanging on to truth and goodness
  And all evils to surmount

Patience is a way of bearing
  Difficulties when they come
Silent peacefulness and blessing
  God's own grace is where it's from

Impatience its opposite
  Leads to turmoil and distress
And a spiral heading down
  To remove our happiness

Kindness is an outward asset
  Friendliness is at its core
Warm regard for those our neighbors
  Gracious goodness to explore

Kindness is benevolence
  Sent to those who are beyond
Not requiring any favor
  From those whom we correspond

Kindness is consideration
  Warm assessment for one's needs
Willingness to reach outside then
  Compensate for other's pleads

Generosity is kindness
  Openness for helping out
Willingness to aid another
  Kindness this without a doubt

Goodness kindness intertwined
  Thus hard to treat them each apart
Goodness though a wider shadow
  Both though coming from the heart

Goodness speaks of pure intentions
  Doing things that thus adhere
Be good do good one's own motto
  Just be sure this is sincere

Good is opposite of evil
  They cannot thus coexist
Live by one but not the other
  Evil thus to be dismissed

Goodness is from God Almighty
  And a grace from God above
When we see it in each other
  Know it comes from God's own love

FRUITS OF THE HOLY SPIRIT - GENEROSITY

Generosity is giving
  Expecting nothing in return
Alms and tithing are examples
  These can be our main concern

Helping others with a smile
  Or expressing gratitude
For a favor not forgotten
  This should be our attitude

Parents raising children do see
  Need to instill charity
Thus to see the needs of others
  Assisting with dexterity

Alms or tithe done regularly
  Seems a never-ending chore
Strangely they give peace and freedom
  More than ever was before

Gentle person wherein lies
  Your secret of tranquility
What about you gives the hint
  Of invulnerability

Gentleness is kept in front
  No need to keep it hidden
Therein lies its golden glow
  A presence not forbidden

With gentleness there is no need
  To posture for the center stage
Gentle giants have a trait
  An inner strength its gauge

Thus in gentleness is strength
  But not a showy kind
Fear and negativity
  Not found in a gentle mind

Faith is trust belief in someone
  Or a thing adherent to
Steadfast and unwavering
  A person or a point of view

Can faith then be misapplied
  As discernment gone awry
What should be our understanding
  Of what to believe and why

Greater love hath no man than
  To give up his life for a friend
Jesus spoke these words for others
  As his life came to its end

Love should be our guide to faith
  With truth and goodness at our side
Faith will then be beautiful
  This we can and should abide

Modesty is being humble
  Of one's attributes and gift
Willingness to share with others
  Praise and not be set adrift

Willingness to share in credit
  Honor and achievement gained
Limiting one's own set portion
  Of what thus has been obtained

There is yet another meaning
  To avoid indecency
And behavior that is prone to
  Indiscretion's guarantee

Modesty entwined with goodness
  And avoidance of extremes
Sharing what one has with others
  And one's truth as conscience deems

FRUITS OF THE HOLY SPIRIT - SELF-CONTROL

Control the power to affect
  Persons or events ahead
Absence of control does lead to
  Peril chaos there instead

Auto driving an example
  Learning when to use the brakes
And obeying traffic lights
  To avoid those big mistakes

Self-control is also needed
  As we live our earthbound life
Goodness conscience truth and beauty
  To transcend this world's strife

We are human help is needed
  Grace from God will lead the way
Surrender prayers to God an answer
  Self-control then here to stay

FRUITS OF THE HOLY SPIRIT - CHASTITY

Chastity begins with family
    Father mother they cause each of us
This a gift from our creator
    Not shared with the angels thus

Father mother share their chastity
    Vow each to the other to refrain
From extramarital sex
    As long as both remain

Boys and girls women and men
    Can and should be chaste as well
Pray the grace from God on high
    Then holiness will help one dwell

Lead a sacramental life
    Baptism confirmation
Penance and the eucharist
    Help maintain this transformation

Canto 9: The Early Church

THE EARLY CHURCH - THE APOSTLES' CREED

The creed of the apostles
  After pentecost was penned
To certify those deep beliefs
  Future christians would defend

Belief in Jesus son of Mary
  Holy Spirit had conceived
Crucified died and was buried
  Then rose thus to be believed

Jesus ascended into heaven
  Sits at the Father's right hand
From thence he will come to judge
  The living and dead as planned

Belief in the holy catholic church
  And the forgiveness of sins
Resurrection of the body
  As life everlasting begins

THE EARLY CHURCH - PETER

Peter the first apostle
  Appointed by Jesus as rock
Upon this rock I will build my church
  And he will then shepherd the flock

After the resurrection
  Peter became the first pope
First in Jerusalem proper
  Then Rome as the christians next hope

Christianity spread and flourished
  Many bishops and priests were named
But trouble arose in the shadows
  A threat that the government claimed

Peter was put into prison
  Then Nero started a fire
Watched Peter being crucified
  Blamed christians for troubles entire

THE EARLY CHURCH - PAUL

Paul a jew and trained pharisee
  Persecutor of the early church
Fell from his horse in blinding light
  And then saw Christ during his lurch

Converting then to Christ's new church
  Paul became a gifted preacher
Especially to the gentiles
  Where he became their teacher

Prolific writer of Christ's scripture
  His to be a rapid rise
Some say equal to St. Peter
  Both in Christ were staunch allies

Arrested and condemned to death
  Sentenced and then moved to Rome
Nero watched while Paul beheaded
  Peter with Paul their final home

Apostle John brother of James
  Picked by Jesus from the cross
To be the new son of Mary
  After John's and Mary's loss

John especially close to Jesus
  Was named the beloved one
Scripture writer the fourth gospel
  And the letters he begun

After Jesus' resurrection
  John with Mary traveled far
The house in Ephesus they lived in
  Visitors come to see from far

All apostles except for John
  Faced a cruel martyr's death
His a graceful older age lived
  Before taking his last breath

The Assumption of Mary
Into heaven after papal search
Has been declared an article
Of faith by the catholic church*

Mary died at age of sixty nine**
And was buried near Jerusalem
Descending from the burial site
Apostles faced a new bedlam

Jesus and his angels in the sky
A vision bearing Mary's soul
They returned to the burial
To understand this vision's goal

Removal of the casket's lid
Revealed that the corpse was gone
Mary's body thus assumed
With her soul was heaven drawn

Source:
*Apostolic Constitution of Pope Pius XII: *Munificentissimus Deus Defining the Dogma of The Assumption*, November 1, 1950

**Venerable Mary of Jesus Agreda, *The Mystical City of God (1670)*, Abridgment, TAN Books, Saint Benedict Press, LLC, Charlotte, North Carolina, 1978, p. 591.

Mother Mary heavenly
  Praised by God the Father thus
Sit at the right hand of thy son
  Nearest there to one of us

Spouse of the Holy Spirit
  And God the Father's daughter
Mother of Jesus the Christ
  The Trinity thus sought her

She has a claim on our dominion
  To my true and natural mother
Queen of creatures we created
  Queen of heaven and all other

Thus was Mary coronated
  Mother of the human race
Each of us should pray to Mary
  Mediatrix of God's grace

Source:
Pius XII: *Encyclical Ad Caeli Reginum*, October 11, 1954
John Paul II: General Audience, July 23, 1997.
Venerable Mary of Jesus Agreda: Op. Cit., p 604.

Longinus the Roman soldier
  Amongst those crucifying Christ
One eye blind received in battle
  Used his lance when it sufficed

Hands on lance and roman short sword
  Reaching up Christ's right side used
Just below the rib cage entered
  Heart was pierced and blood then oozed

Blood splashed on Longinus' blind eye
  Former sight was then restored
Later baptized then a deacon
  Later martyred for his Lord

Father forgive they do not know
  Jesus said while on the cross
This applied to Longinus
  As he regained his visual loss

Adrian roman commander
Then of the Praetorian Guard
Of the emperor Diocletian
Duties that he soon found hard

Christians for their faith were martyred
Cruel they were torn and gored
Cheerful singing for each other
Him this could not be ignored

Adrian became a convert
Of this nascent christian faith
Stop this nonsense said his captors
It will disappear a wraith

Adrian was executed
As were thousands of his peers
Yet this new religion flourished
Expanding in future years

Catholic means universal
  Apt name for the christian church
Christ himself did first imply this
  With his teaching and our search

The apostle's creed a source*
  Catholic church St. Matthew said
Each apostle spoke a symbol
  With St. Peter at the head

St. Ignatius of Antioch
  First century patriarch
Early on called the church catholic
  Recognized as a benchmark

Ignatius then went on to Rome
  And received a martyr's crown
In the footsteps of St. Peter
  Martyred in the selfsame town

 Source:
*Venerable Mary of Jesus Agreda, Op. Cit., p 506.

Jesus summoned the apostles
  Telling them what they should do
Made a circuit of villages
  Teaching telling what he knew

Sending them out two by two
  Instructing them to take nothing
For the journey but a staff
  In their going and their coming

Power over unclean spirits
  Theirs to use as they saw fit
Bring no wallet bread or money
  Stay wherever they permit

Whoever does not listen to you
  Leave that house and go away
Shake the dust from off your sandals
  As a witness your display

The christian mass was introduced
  During the first century
About the time the catholic church
  Became the documentary

Scripture and the words of Christ
  Form the essence of the mass
Testaments both old and new
  Read as they have come to pass

Bread and wine at consecration
  Become Christ's body and his blood
This the transubstantiation
  God's grace pours as with a flood

Eat my body drink my blood
  Eucharist to eat and drink
Christ today as centuries past
  This our spiritual link

Pray always for this grace from God
　For what we need for those we love
For even those we do not know
　Our constant help from God above

Then God will shed his love as grace
　To all of those who pray for it
For even those who do not pray
　He loves us all he does commit

Then grace from God and prayer from us
　Become a language to and fro
This language love so powerful
　Becomes a language we should know

Love is from God God is love
　And we possess capacity
To use this power God provides
　A sign of God's sagacity

THE EARLY CHURCH - PRAYERS

Jesus gave us the Lord's prayer
  Instruction as to how to pray
Honoring our Father God
  All the words and what to say

Hail Mary full of grace
  First appeared in Luke's good news
Holy Mary the second verse
  Ninth century used in the pews

The glory be fourth century
  The creed during apostles' time
St. Dominic gave the rosary
  Reflections on Christ's life sublime

Many memorize these prayers
  Reciting from an early age
But contemplation thoughts not words
  A beautiful way to so engage

Who is this Mary talked about
  Pre-christian Jewish maiden sure
Background hidden humble pure
  Otherwise a girl obscure

Many other girls out there
  With qualities that would suffice
Yet for salvation to begin
  Humanity must pay the price

Mary's soul immaculate
  Thus free from the original sin
And although Mary one of us
  She was from God unique within

Mother daughter spouse as one
  Queen of heaven then to be
Advocate for humanity
  Conduit for God's grace is she

THE EARLY CHURCH - POPES

The papal legacy began
  With Peter for whom Jesus said
Thou art Peter and upon this rock
  I will build my church the scripture read

Five popes spanned the first century
  Following Lord Jesus birth
Peter Linus Anacletus
  The first three upon the earth

Clement I and Evaristus
  Were the two popes next in line
All were saints and some were martyrs
  Line unbroken God's design

Two hundred sixty-six the number
  Popes in one continuous flow
From Peter up to Francis current
  Faith in this we do thus show

These are thirty-six all told
  Doctors of the catholic church
All are saints and recognized
  For their theological search

Ambrose Augustine and Jerome
  With Anastasia the first
All named during twelve ninety-eight
  Profound statements they had versed

Teresa of Avila
  With Therese of Lisieux
And Catherine of Siena
  Women doctors for review

These doctors through two thousand years
  Contributed immensely to
The knowledge gained about the faith
  Truth for others to pursue

Canto 10: Sacraments

SACRAMENTS OF THE CHURCH - BAPTISM

John the Baptist Jesus' cousin
  Said be baptized to be saved
Using water from the Jordan
  Many baptized which they craved

Jesus came and said baptize me
  John complied let water spread
This is my beloved son
  Listen to him Father said

Water oil priest and patron
  I baptize thee in the name
Father Son and Holy Spirit
  Thence forth sealed is God's claim

Sacrament of new conversion
  Soul is cleansed sin washed away
Grace with joy and peace can enter
  Truth and goodness on display

Parents bring their little ones
  As well as those of any age
Before the age of reasoning
  For baptism's initial stage

But confirmation has its place
  To certify the truth therein
Those baptized of every age
  Learn and let their faith begin

Confirmation has its rite
  A bishop laying on of hands
Lifelong grace is thus bestowed
  And the confirmed then understands

Special are the graces that
  This sacrament has thus bestowed
The Holy Spirits gifts and fruits
  Are precious and to God are owed

Penance is that sacrament
    Removing future sin from us
Enter the confessional
    And ask forgiveness no further fuss

An extension of baptism
    Sin committed since that time
Priest then gives Christ's absolution
    Grace from God that is sublime

Penitents finish with a prayer
    Of sorrow and remorse for sin
Joy and peace do follow this
    Wondrous feelings deep within

But I pity the poor priest
    Sitting in and listening to
Sins he's heard thousands of times
    A stuffy place until he's through

Mass the holy sacrifice
  That faithful masses do attend
Eucharist entwined within
  The liturgy does thus depend

This is my body this my blood
  Selfsame words that Jesus said
Repeated by the priest at mass
  Consecrating wine and bread

At each moment round the world
  Masses offered to the Lord
People from each land attend
  And encompass one accord

Eat my body drink my blood
  Words that Jesus spoke that night
Holy eucharist all partake
  Communicating with delight

SACRAMENTS OF THE CHURCH -
ANOINTING OF THE SICK

The ailing and the aging have
  A sacrament applied to them
Suffering associated
  Blessing does assuage and stem

Illness carries certain pangs
  Closure anguish and despair
The sacrament provides a prayer
  Calm acceptance grace to bear

A priest applies the oil blessed
  To the forehead and the hands
Of one suffering age or ill
  As the sacrament commands

Know what this sacrament can do
  A special blessing for the soul
Peace and comfort it can bring
  While age and illness take their toll

Church the vehicle of Christ on earth
  Sanctifies the pairing of each two
Man and woman bound together
  In the vow they both hold true

Bride and groom themselves give birth
  To their vow before a priest
Each to other throughout life
  Until death or circumstance has ceased

Two the start of family
  Then anger petulance and strife
Human traits so prevalent
  Enter threaten married life

This sacrament teaches the two
  To pray together for God's grace
For buoyancy to keep intact
  Their marriage and its close embrace

Sacrament of Holy Orders
  Where to go for further search
Jesus stated thou art Peter
  Upon this rock I build my church

Bishops priests and deacons are
  Persons consecrated then and now
Peter then became the pope
  The church continues to endow

Vocations only God bestows
  Years of training supervision
Then the bishop consecrates
  A Priest for life this joint decision

The church is one and apostolic
  Also catholic and holy
These with Holy Orders mark
  The church entire and wholly

TEACHING OF THE CHURCH - SIN

What is sin that we should know
　First an offense against God
Our first parents were the first
　To venture on this path so odd

Their first sin was disobeying
　God's explicit command thus
Punishment was swift and certain
　Banishment and death for us

Evils we confront and fail to
　So avoid and put aside
They control us take our freedom
　Leave us sentenced in our pride

Grievous matter full reflection
　And consent of the free will
Sin will enter full upon us
　Penance used will cleanse it still

Canto 11: Teaching of the Church's Virtues

THE CHURCH'S THEOLOGICAL VIRTUE - FAITH

Faith a disposition of the mind
 With heart and soul a firm belief
Of things eternal and divine
 A splendor and sublime motif

Faith is of God placed there for us
 Like conscience meant a guide to be
Given in great love for us
 Given by the Triune Three

Faith informs our inner selves
 Of how we relate to God
Truth and certainty is ours
 We do not need a further prod

When tested faith provides the strength
 To persist despite cost and pain
Martyrs in the early church
 Gave their all for heavenly gain

Hope a disposition of the mind
  With heart and soul a third attend
Of things eternal and divine
  Things that we do comprehend

Hope teaches to place our trust
  In God for all our future needs
Calm acceptance we pursue
  Molding of our future deeds

Hope denies a space for fear
  Saying do not be afraid
Jesus gave this same advice
  While on earth for us He prayed

Hope is paired with surrender
  Fearlessly to God in trust
God takes care of every thing
  When we live right and be just

Charity a disposition
  Mind and heart and soul portend
Source divine and thus eternal
  Command from God as from a friend

Charity is love from God
  Extended as His love for us
Meant to be shared ever widely
  Humankind's most needed plus

Charity cannot be contained
  When released it reaches far
To another then another
  As the distance to a star

Charity when kept within us
  Does no harm to any one
Peace and joy for self and others
  Force that cannot be undone

THE CHURCH'S CARDINAL VIRTUE: PRUDENCE

Prudence is that virtue which asks
  Questions which should come to mind
Questions that address uncertainty
  And kept closely intertwined

Frivolity is not the kind
  Of questions that do here apply
But questions needing common sense
  For answers here that do supply

These are question dealing with
  The daily do's and don'ts of life
Answers that retain the good
  And forestall evil's future strife

Prudence seeks the answers wisdom gives
  Seeking council from the truly wise
Patient waiting for solutions
  Finding solace for the prize

Justice means obedience
  To the just laws that we live by
Of accountability
  In jurisdictions that apply

But justice has a moral tone
  Of conscience and the rules of God
Render unto others with love
  What is needed not so odd

Justice guides relationships
  And the balance struck between
Selfishness and selflessness
  And the neighbor's needs foreseen

Justice speaks of fair dealings
  And charity towards neighbors
Rendering what should be done
  With holdings and with labors

Fortitude is bravery
  Bravery for every day
Courage for the daily throes
  That could lead us far astray

Fortitude is steadiness
  A moral virtue seeking good
Separating what we should not
  And indicating what we should

There is the bravery that shields
  Soldiers fighting battles in war
Ribbons medals and parades
  Bands and crowd's acclaiming roar

But fortitude is something else
  A single mother with two jobs
Overworked yet steadfast keeping
  Family between her sobs

Like other virtues Temperance
Seeks the good in what we do
It is that moral building block
For beauty good and what is true

Temperance is mastery
Of our nature's base intentions
Habits using good and pleasant
To offset evil's pretensions

Temperance is self-restraint
The use of moderation
Placing first the good and true
For every situation

From foods we eat to use of sex
Maintain a moral focus
Avoid those tendencies we face
Like games of hocus-pocus

Canto 12: The Afterlife

THE CHURCH'S FINAL FOUR - DEATH

Death carries finality
  For each and every one of us
At a time we may not know
  And despite the fume and fuss

Sometimes is anticipated
  As with illness and of age
Other times is of a sudden
  Taking life at any stage

We should carefully think of death
  Its effect on us and those
Family members and the others
  Lives entwined as nature flows

Special thought for what will follow
  Afterlife in all its forms
Live life keeping God as central
  And adhering to his norms

The church avers two judgements
 Before beginning the last climb
One immediately after death
 The other at the end of time

After death our God will judge us
 Based on how we've lived our lives
Sin the nexus that determines
 Our afterlife and how derived

The second judgement coincides
 With Jesus' return to the world
All those living and the deceased
 Will be judged with sins unfurled

Follow forgive love all others
 Do not be afraid he said
Jesus told us not to worry
 He saves living and the dead

Time our tether to our bosom earth
  But at the end of time what then
Surely timelessness for each
  Into eternity amen

Experiences of near death
  From those who then recover
Find light and peace and pleasantness
  A tunnel they discover

Heaven is the destination
  For souls not enmeshed in sin
Glory and tranquility
  With God and all and with one's kin

We cannot know only surmise
  What the life in heaven will be
Joined with bodies resurrected
  Glorious forever free

There are no atheists in hell
Fallen angels devils know
And so do humans banished
To those caverns far below

Hate for God these banished share
Deep foreboding loathing's hurt
Fire other pains do not
The primacy of hate divert

Yet what will lead these souls to hell
Sin so vast encompassed so
Sinner's pride that banishes
Salvation's path for souls to go

Judgement between life and death
May forestall hell's deep abyss
Fatima provides a prayer*
For mercy and God's loving kiss

*Oh my Jesus forgive us our sins save us from the fires of
hell, lead all souls to heaven and help especially those most
in need of Thy mercy.

THE CHURCH: PURGATORY

Not included in the final four
  Purgatory is a holding place
For purging of remaining sins
  Thus a hopeful waiting space

There is fire for souls to bear
  As punishment or cleansing
But hope abounds for all those there
  Of future peace commencing

Purgatory filled with love
  Of God and one another
Hate dispelled there is no room
  Love treats all like a brother

Souls in purgatory know
  That heaven will be later
Prayers for souls in purgatory
  May speed the time made straighter

Epilogue

The word church resounds like a drumbeat through these writings. Surely there are multiple meanings. Bricks and mortar surrounding places of worship are a common meaning; but this is not what these writings are about.

And what of that startup Jesus? He picked Simon, a quite ordinary person, changed his name to Peter, and said: "Thou art Peter, and upon this rock I will build my church, and the gates of hell shall not prevail against it." Who is it that changes another person's name? Who is it that would allow one's name to be changed? What ordinary person would allow such a lofty definition be applied to him? And who of Simon Peter's associates would accept this without question? Only God knows. And God knew. Jesus is the Word, the Son of God, the Second person of the Trinity. Jesus knew, and his words were not then questioned.

After Peter, the church became Christian. Yet, Jesus applied a larger meaning when he said: "I do not pray for these alone, but also for those who will believe in me through their word; that they all may be one, as You, Father, are one in me, and I in You; that they may also be one in Us, that the world may believe that You sent me." (John 17:20-23). Thus, church applies to the people of God; but who are these people?

Since all people come from our creator God, church, in this sense, applies to all.

Of the three monotheistic religions: Hebrew, Christian, and Islam, all acknowledge Jesus, but in different ways. Jesus was Jewish, as were his mother Mary, his foster father Joseph, and the majority of his followers. They regarded him as the Messiah, the promised deliverer in the Hebrew Bible. Jews were converted and baptized, by the thousands, during Pentecost.

Islam was founded by Muhammad in the sixth and seventh centuries. The holy book of Islam, the *Quran*, includes Abraham, Jacob (Israel), Ishmael (Islam), and Jesus (Christian) in its pages. Jesus was placed among the greatest of the prophets of Allah (God), along with many from the Hebrew Bible. Of particular note, the *Quran* regards Jesus as Messiah, as the Son of God, the Word of God, and as being born of a virgin.*

Thus there seems to be more in common among the varied churches and religions than separate us; differences similar to sibling rivalry, but on a much larger scale. Jesus also provided the great commandment of Love, first of God, then of neighbor as self. Jesus seems to imply that neighbor means everyone else.

We may thus suggest the daily saying of the Lord's Prayer, by ourselves and all others; said with love, by members of all religions and churches; and intended for all mankind.

Our Father (Yahweh, Allah) who art in heaven
Hallowed (Holy) be Thy Name
Thy kingdom come, Thy will be done
On earth as it is in Heaven
Give us this day our daily bread
And forgive us our trespasses
As we forgive those who trespass against us
And lead us not into temptation
But deliver us from evil
For thine is the kingdom and the power
And the glory now and forever. Amen

Source:
*Quran in English, Talal Itani (Translator). Publisher: Clear Quran, Plano Texas, May 20th, 2020. ps: 3,7,9,10,17,52.